X-RAY DINOSAURS
AND OTHER PREHISTORIC CREATURES

Susan R. Stoltz   illustrated by Cody Hooper-Kaufmann

edited by Sandi K. Drewitz

For my friend Deborah
who knows that dinosaurs are the best!

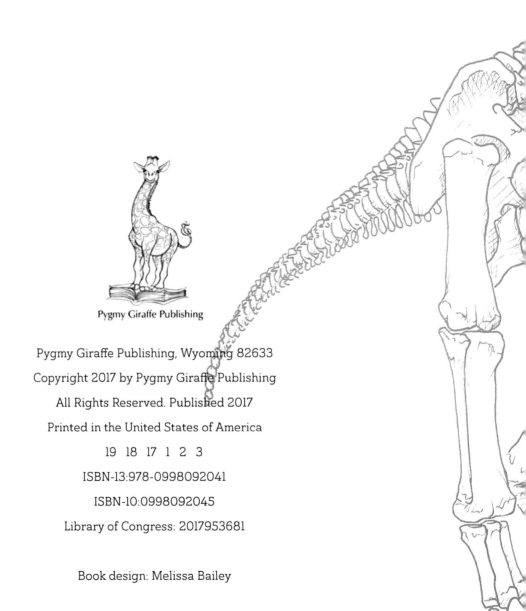

Pygmy Giraffe Publishing

Pygmy Giraffe Publishing, Wyoming 82633

Copyright 2017 by Pygmy Giraffe Publishing

All Rights Reserved. Published 2017

Printed in the United States of America

19 18 17 1 2 3

ISBN-13:978-0998092041

ISBN-10:0998092045

Library of Congress: 2017953681

Book design: Melissa Bailey

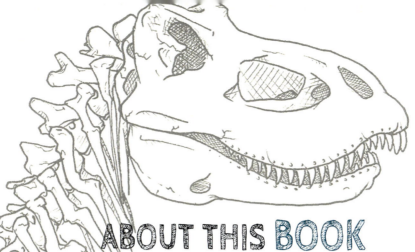

ABOUT THIS BOOK

There aren't many animals in the world that can compete with the sheer magnificence, size, and variety of dinosaurs, pterosaurs, plesiosaurs, and other prehistoric creatures. Although their descendants are alive on earth today, not much is known about what these animals looked like, their habits and behavior, or the reason for their extinction. In fact, what we know about them is miniscule in comparison to what we DON'T know.

As we continue to unearth their remains, our knowledge base expands and changes, which makes the art of quoting fact a very fluid task. In other words, the scientific data changes so rapidly that it's difficult to keep up. The information in this book is stated to the best of my knowledge and with the assistance of a very helpful paleontologist, Robert McCord, from the Arizona Natural History Museum. His patience and input were most appreciated.

The watercolors in these illustrations are rather fanciful. Although we have little clue as to the actual colors of these prehistoric creatures, we are relatively certain they would have blended in with their jungle, water, or arid environments. Predator or prey status also would have influenced coloration.

Be inspired! Use your imagination when thinking about these magnificent creatures that once roamed the earth.

Archaeopteryx was the first bird discovered.
Her fossil was the first feathered imprints uncovered.
Eighteen inches in length, she had wings sprouting claws,
To help scramble up branches. She had teeth in her jaws!

ARCHAEOPTERYX

ARK-ee-OP-turr-icks

Geographical Location: Germany

Length: 18"

Diet: Carnivore

Age: Late Jurassic

Biped/Winged

TYRANNOSAURUS REX

tye-RAN-oh-SORE-us REX
Geographical Location: North America
Length: 40'
Diet: Carnivore
Age: Late Cretaceous
Biped

He was fast, he was big, the scariest of all.
Tyrannosaurus rex was 20 feet tall.
With wee little arms and teeth that crushed bone,
The *Tyrant Lizard King* is very well known.

TRICERATOPS

tri-SERR-uh-tops

Geographical Location: North America

Length: 30'

Diet: Herbivore

Age: Late Cretaceous

Quadruped

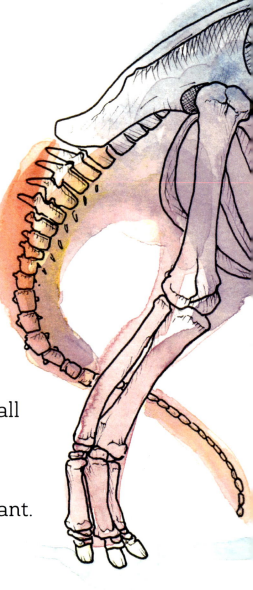

The prize for the largest dino head of them all
Belongs to the Triceratops' eight-foot skull.
Built like a rhino, but as big as an elephant,
Her four-foot long horns were never irrelevant.

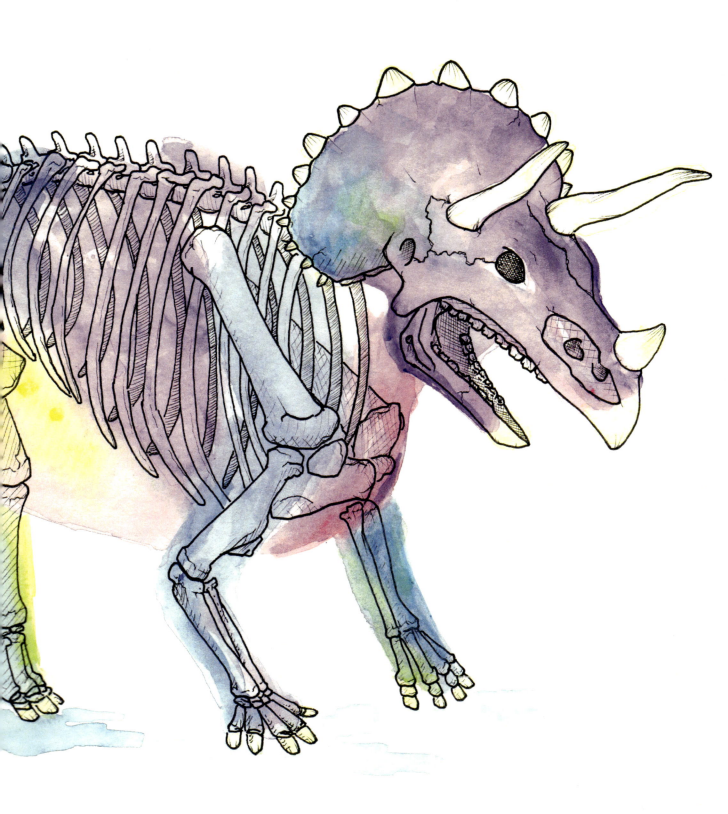

DIMORPHODON

di-MOR-fo-don

Geographical Location: England, Mexico

Length: 8'

Diet: Carnivore

Age: Mid Jurassic

Quadruped/Winged

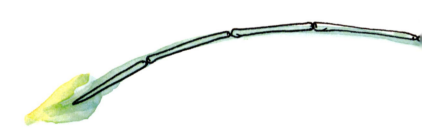

A gigantic head for a dino that flew,
Dimorphodon had two kinds of teeth and could chew.
One was for grabbing, the other to grind.
He was about as funny looking as any ptero you'd find.

Psittacosaurus had a parrot-like beak,
Bristles on her tail and horns on her cheeks.
She was covered in scales of various sizes.
Dinosaur fossils are FULL of surprises!

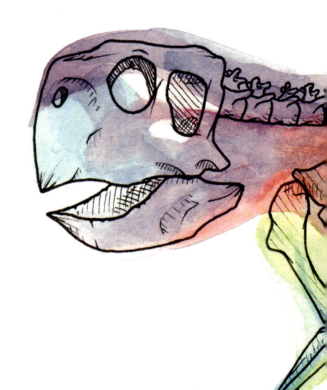

PSITTACOSAURUS

SIT-ah-co-SORE-us

Geographical Location: China

Length: 6.5'

Diet: Herbivore

Age: Cretaceous

Biped

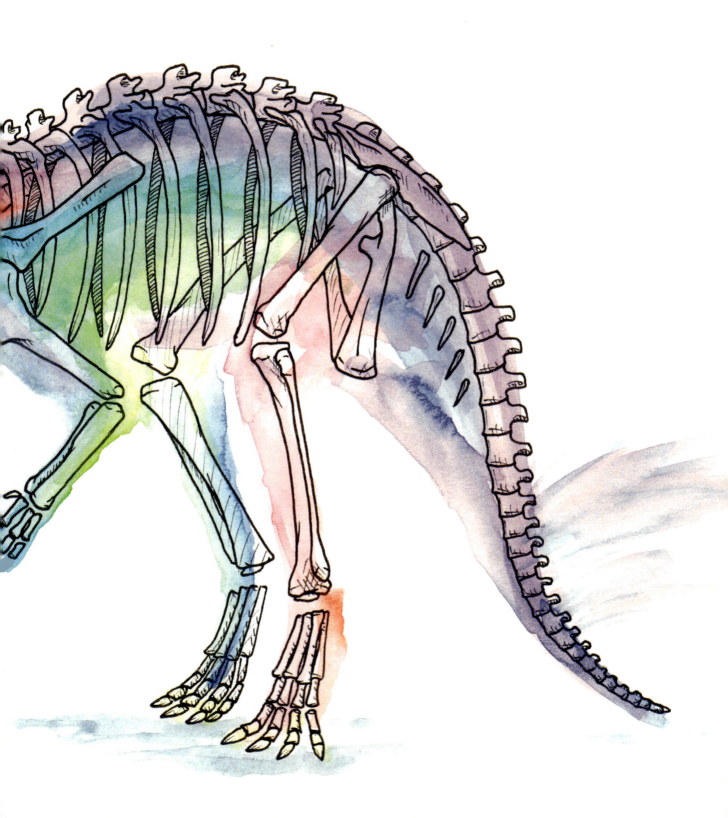

PARASAUROLOPHUS

PAR-ah-saw-RAH-loh-fuss

Geographical Location: North America

Length: 31'

Diet: Herbivore

Age: Late Cretaceous

Quadruped

Parasaurolophus had tubes in her head.
Either she had to cool off or was musical instead.
Scientists aren't certain if she used them to call,
Or if they regulated her body temperature overall!

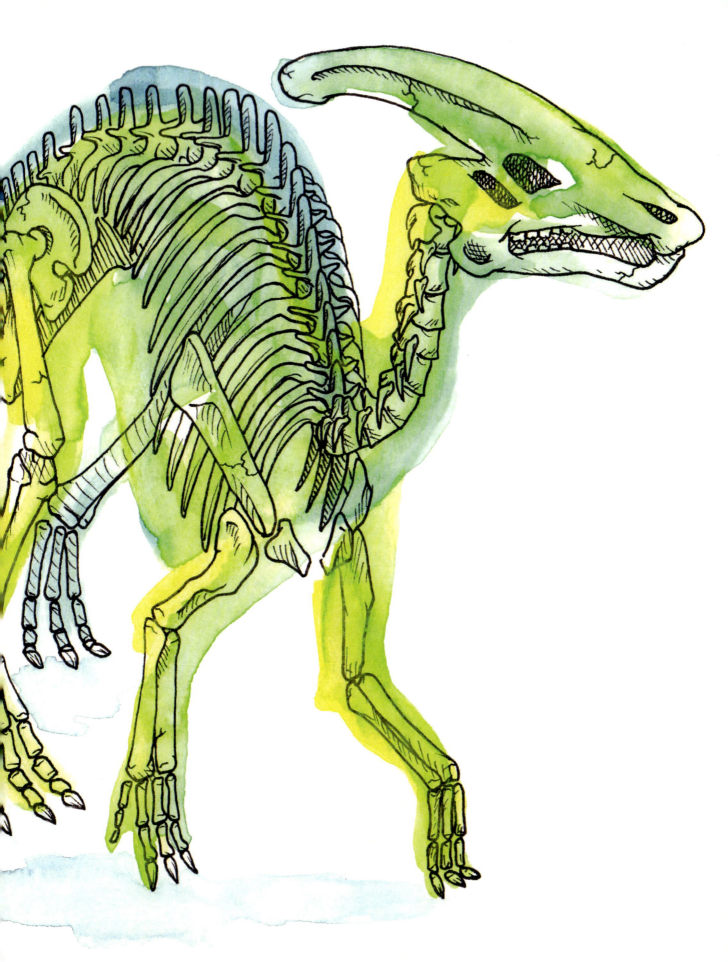

GIRAFFATITAN

jih-RAFF-ah-tie-tan

Geographical Location: Africa

Length: 80' – 85'

Diet: Herbivore

Age: Late Jurassic

Quadruped

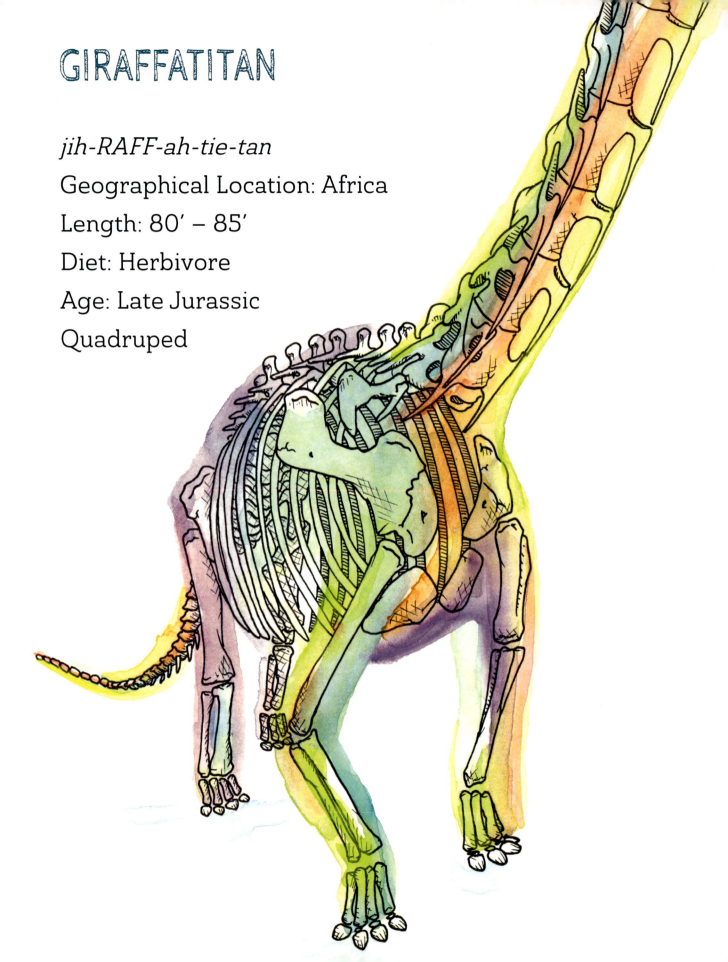

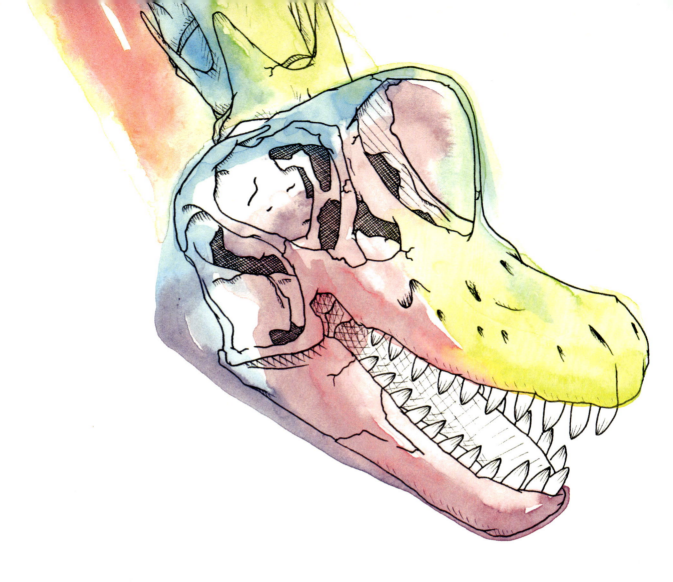

Giraffatitan reached 49 feet in the air.
To look in his eye you'd need 84 stairs!
Large circular feet helped him stand steady and tall.
For something so large, his tail was quite small.

LIOPLEURODON

lie-oh-PLOOR-oh-don

Geographical Location: Oceans

Length: 22' – 25'

Diet: Carnivore

Age: Jurassic

Aquatic

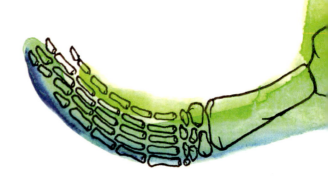

Here's a neat trick you should never try ever.
Liopleurodon could smell underwater. How clever!
A fast, strong swimmer with super large nostrils,
She had bunches of teeth that show up in the fossils.

GASTORNIS

gas-TORN-us

Geographical Location: North America, Europe

Length: 6'

Diet: Unknown

Age: Early Cenozoic

Biped

About the size of an ostrich but so much more sturdy,
Gastornis had a big head, a huge giant birdy.
His beak was quite large, his wings super small.
He relied on his feet, did not fly at all.

MOSASAURUS

mos-a-SORE-us

Geographical Location: Oceans
Length: 56'
Diet: Carnivore
Age: Late Cretaceous
Aquatic

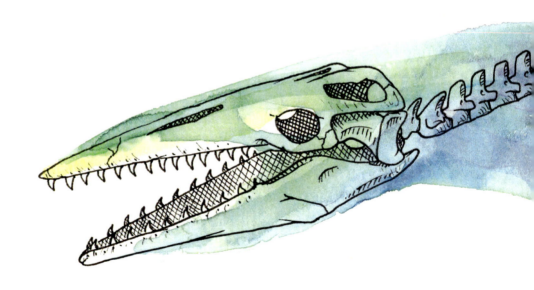

Mosasaurus wasn't a fish, you see.
He had to breathe air just like you and like me.
To think he's a plesiosaur is a preconceived notion.
He's considered a reptile that lived in the ocean.

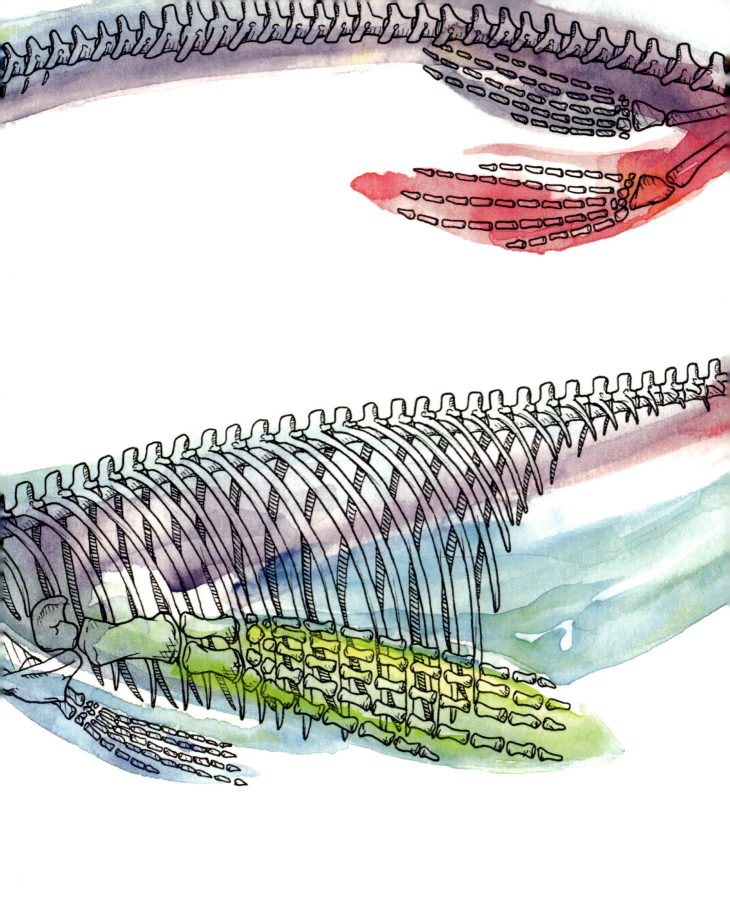

PACHYCEPHALOSAURUS

pack-ih-SEF-ah-low-SORE-us

Geographical Location: North America

Length: 16'

Diet: Herbivore

Age: Late Cretaceous

Biped

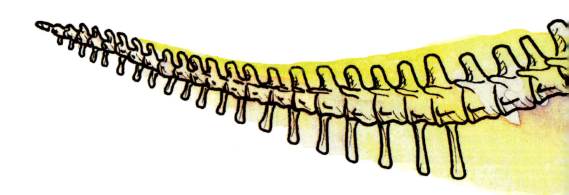

Pachycephalosaurus, seven syllables it is.
Her head was 10 inches thick – what a lid!
Her eyes were set forward, her vision was good.
Why her head was so thick is not understood.

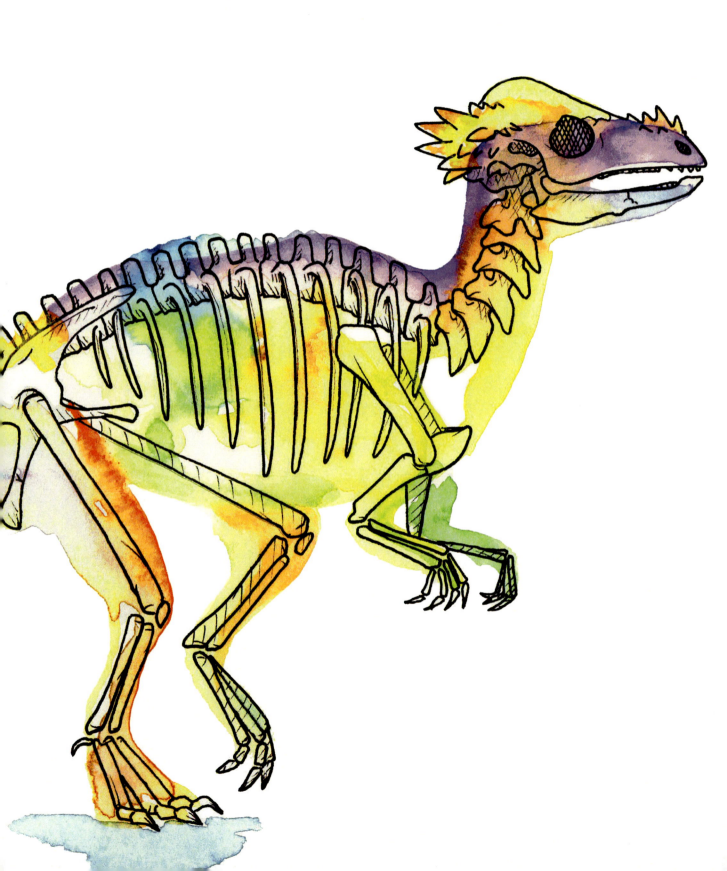

CITIPATI

CHITT-i-putt-ee

Geographical Location: Asia

Length: 10'

Diet: Omnivore

Age: Cretaceous

Biped

Closely related to birds, Citipati had feathers.
From head down to feet, he was warm in cold weather.
He had great big hands and a beak with no teeth,
A crest on his head and strong claws on his feet.

TARCHIA

TAHR-key-ah
Geographical Location: Mongolia, Asia
Length: 26' – 28'
Diet: Herbivore
Age: Late Cretaceous
Quadruped

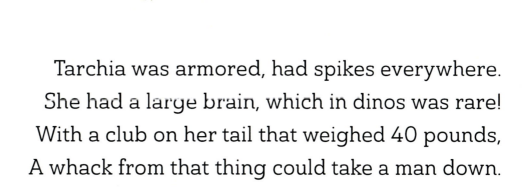

Tarchia was armored, had spikes everywhere.
She had a large brain, which in dinos was rare!
With a club on her tail that weighed 40 pounds,
A whack from that thing could take a man down.

UTAHRAPTOR

YOO-tah-RAP-tor

Geographical Location: Utah, United States

Length: 19.5'

Diet: Carnivore

Age: Early Cretaceous

Biped

Utahraptor, the biggest raptor of all.
On the second toe was a nine-inch claw.
He could jump 15 feet, run 20 miles per hour.
His razor sharp teeth were made to devour!

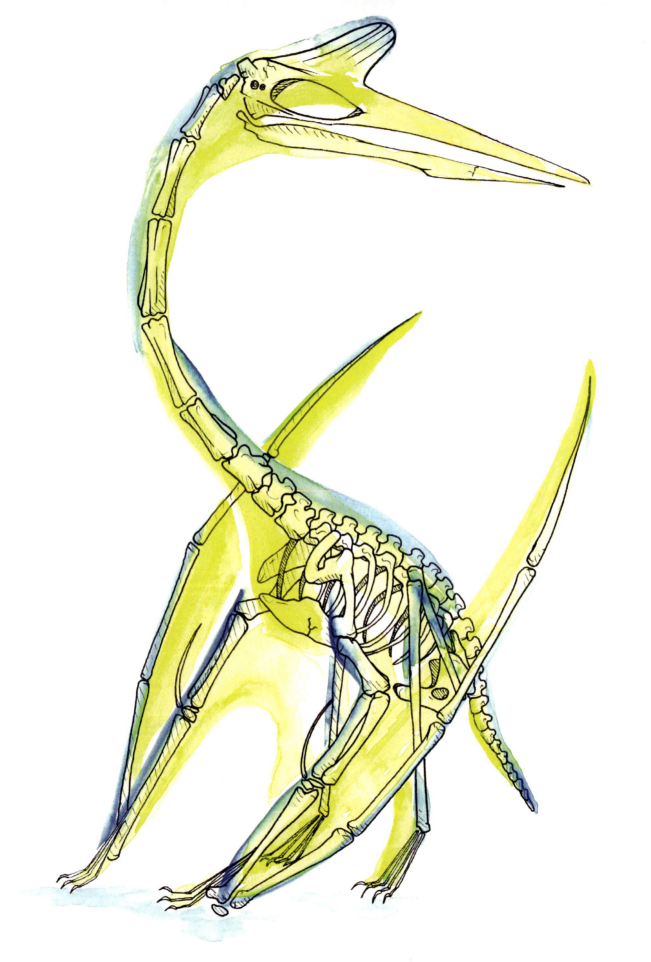

QUETZALCOATLUS

kwet-SAL-co-AT-lus

Geographical Location: Texas, United States

Wingspan: 33'

Diet: Carnivore

Age: Late Cretaceous

Quadruped/Winged

Quetzalcoatlus was as tall as a giraffe.
His wings were as wide as a small aircraft!
He had a big beak and no teeth at all,
Swallowed dinosaurs whole, but they had to be small.

The Stegosaurus had plates up his spine.
Triangular they ran up both sides looking fine.
His tail a harsh blow could really deliver.
Elaborately decorated, he's called the *Roofed Lizard*.

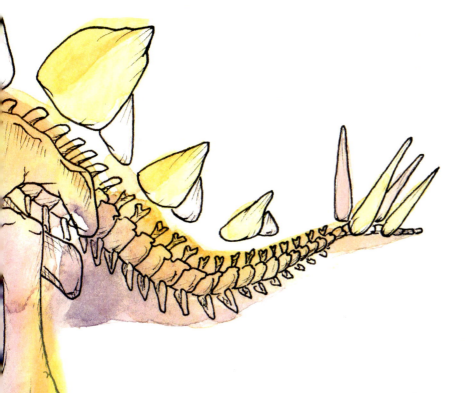

STEGOSAURUS

STEG-oh-SORE-us
Geographical Location: North America
Length: 30'
Diet: Herbivore
Age: Late Jurassic
Quadruped

Dilophosaurus had a crest like a hat.
Arizona was his Jurassic habitat.
His bony head crest didn't have any frill,
But he did have sharp teeth that could easily kill.

DILOPHOSAURUS

die-LOFF-ah-SORE-us

Geographical Location: Arizona, United States

Length: 20' – 23'

Diet: Carnivore

Age: Early Jurassic

Biped

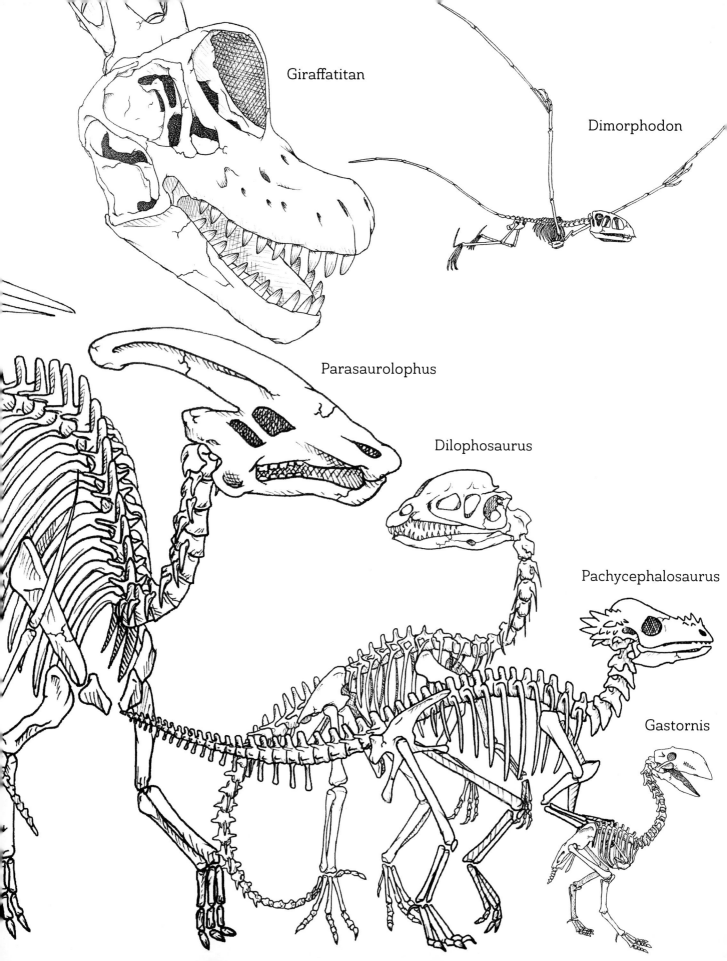

GLOSSARY OF TERMS

Biped – an animal that uses two legs for walking.

Carnivore – an animal that eats meat. Most meat eaters have sharper teeth to tear meat rather than flat teeth to grind plants.

Cenozoic Era – a span of geological time, which occurred 65 million years ago to the present day and included two periods: the Tertiary and Quaternary Periods.

Cretaceous Period – the third period of the Mesozoic Era of geological time, which occurred 65 - 145 million years ago.

Dinosaur – a carnivorous or herbivorous reptile that lived during the Mesozoic Era and is now extinct.

Extinction – when a form of life comes to an end.

Fossil – can be a track, bone, plant, insect, or body part that is preserved by being covered with mud or sand. This allows minerals to enter the fossil and harden it.

Geological Time – Earth's history, broken into eras and periods.

Herbivore – animals that eat plants. Most plant eaters have flatter teeth to grind plants rather than sharp pointed teeth to tear meat.

Jurassic Period – the second period of the Mesozoic Era of geological time, which occurred 145 - 200 million years ago.

Mammal – a warm blooded vertebrate that produces milk to feed the young, that has hair or fur, and that (typically) gives birth to live babies. Humans are mammals.

Mesozoic Era – a span of geological time, which occurred 65 - 250 million years ago and included three periods: Triassic, Jurassic, and Cretaceous.

Paleontology – a science that deals with the life of past geological periods as known from fossil remains. A scientist who studies paleontology is a paleontologist.

Plesiosaur – a large marine reptile, with paddle-like limbs and a long flexible neck, that lived during the Mesozoic Era and is now extinct.

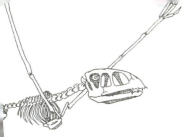

GLOSSARY OF TERMS

Predator – a meat-eating animal that hunts other animals for food.

Prey – an animal that is hunted by other animals for food.

Pterosaur – a flying reptile that lived during the Mesozoic Era and is now extinct.

Quadruped – an animal that uses four legs for walking.

Skeleton – bone or cartilage that is the support structure of an animal.

Triassic Period – the first period of the Mesozoic Era of geological time, which occurred 200 - 250 million years ago.

Vertebrate – an animal that has a backbone or spinal column.

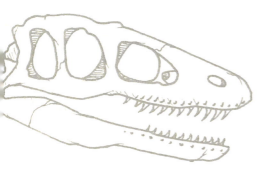

BIBLIOGRAPHY

Lessem, Dom. *The Ultimate Dino-Pedia — The Most Complete Dinosaur Reference Ever.* Washington, DC: National Geographic Partners, 2010.

Paul, Gregory S. *The Princeton Field Guide to Dinosaurs.* 2nd ed. New Jersey: Princeton University Press, 2016.

Pim, Keiron. *Dinosaurs — the Grand Tour: Everything Worth Knowing about Dinosaurs from Aardonyx to Zuniceratops.* With field notes by Jack Horner. New York: The Experiment, 2016.

Smithsonian. *Dinosaur! Dinosaurs and Other Amazing Prehistoric Creatures as You've Never Seen Them Before.* New York: DK Publishing, 2014.

ABOUT THE CONTRIBUTORS

Susan R. Stoltz has several published works and currently concentrates on children's books. With a varied career in journalism, editing, children's books, and autobiography, Susan currently works at the Phoenix Zoo and enjoys teaching people of all ages about the amazing and diverse wildlife on the planet. She lives with her Jack Russell terrier and Siamese cat.

Cody Hooper-Kaufmann polished his skills at the Academy of Art University. In 2015, he focused on his love of animals and his passion for whimsical ink-and-watercolor painting to start his own art business, HeArt by Cody. He shares his Vancouver, Washington home with three adorable but rather pushy cats and a red-tailed boa named Zora.

Sandi K. Drewitz edits children's books, novels, nonfiction books, and technical documentation. She recently retired from the Phoenix Zoo and looks forward to new adventures. She shares her home in Scottsdale, Arizona with her family and two very chatty parrots.

BOOKS BY PYGMY GIRAFFE PUBLISHING

 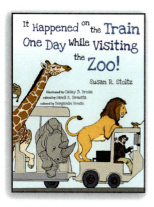  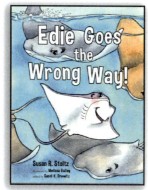

Available for purchase online at Amazon.com.

COMING SOON!

Totter the Otter

Hop-Along Saves the Day

A Galaxy, a Smack, and a Shiver

There's Something You Can Do

The Snotty Coati

Curriculum is available for *X-Ray Dinosaurs*. This unit contains nine different lessons to be used in kindergarten through fourth grade classrooms, aligned with National Common Core Literacy Standards.

Please visit www.pygmygiraffepublishing.com for purchase information.

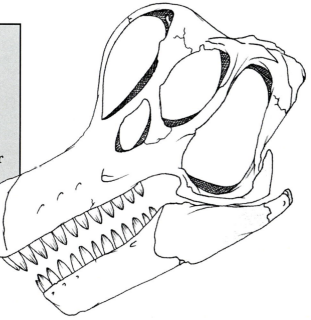

Made in the USA
San Bernardino, CA
22 December 2017